The European Union Today
A Quest for Unity Amidst Diversity

Thomas M. Magstadt
Rockhurst College

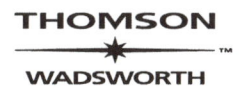

THOMSON
WADSWORTH

Australia • Canada • Mexico • Singapore • Spain • United Kingdom • United States

COPYRIGHT © 2004 Wadsworth, a division of Thomson Learning, Inc. Thomson Learning™ is a trademark used herein under license.

ALL RIGHTS RESERVED. No part of this work covered by the copyright hereon may be reproduced or used in any form or by any means—graphic, electronic, or mechanical, including but not limited to photocopying, recording, taping, Web distribution, information networks, or information storage and retrieval systems—without the written permission of the publisher.

Printed in Canada
1 2 3 4 5 6 7   07 06 05 04 03

Printer: Transcontinental Printing

0-534-64341-8

For more information about our products, contact us at:
Thomson Learning Academic Resource Center
1-800-423-0563

For permission to use material from this text, contact us by:
Phone: 1-800-730-2214
Fax: 1-800-731-2215
Web: http://www.thomsonrights.com

Wadsworth/Thomson Learning
10 Davis Drive
Belmont, CA 94002-3098
USA

Asia
Thomson Learning
5 Shenton Way #01-01
UIC Building
Singapore 068808

Australia/New Zealand
Thomson Learning
102 Dodds Street
Southbank, Victoria 3006
Australia

Canada
Nelson
1120 Birchmount Road
Toronto, Ontario M1K 5G4
Canada

Europe/Middle East/South Africa
Thomson Learning
High Holborn House
50/51 Bedford Row
London WC1R 4LR
United Kingdom

Latin America
Thomson Learning
Seneca, 53
Colonia Polanco
11560 Mexico D.F.
Mexico

Spain/Portugal
Paraninfo
Calle/Magallanes, 25
28015 Madrid, Spain

The European Union Today:
A Quest for Unity Amidst Diversity

Table of Contents

Preface	2
Introduction	2
What Europeans Share	4
A Culture of Liberty	7
The Expectation of Prosperity	8
A Cherished Diversity	12
A Desire for Unity	17
Ambivalence Toward EU Authority	21
Europe and America	30
Summary and Conclusions	36
Select Bibliography	40
Notes	41

Preface

This booklet is intended to accompany and supplement Part II of my textbook, *Nations and Governments: Comparative Politics in Regional Perspective.* The reader is encouraged to read it in conjunction with Chapter 4, "The Triumph of Parliaments and Pluralism" – especially pages 165-172. Of course, I am aware that it might also be used by itself or with other instructional materials, and have tried to write it a way that will reflect that awareness and facilitate multiple uses. Whether or not I have succeeded is for you, the reader, to decide.

Introduction

The idea of a unified Europe, as opposed to a Europe of nations, is not new. In fact, it has been the pet project of many of Europe's most illustrious thinkers – not to mention an assortment of dreamers and schemers – for centuries.[1] In the mid-1960s, after the Common Market had become a reality but before it had expanded beyond the original Six, a noted scholar wrote, "It has been possible to unify France, Germany, and Italy, but not Europe, and not even Austria-Hungary. The organizing principle of modern Europe has not been the unity of federalism, but the independence of nationalism."[2]

Nationalism acquired a bad name in the twentieth century as a result of two shockingly destructive world wars; its association with right-wing totalitarianism in Germany, Italy and elsewhere; and, finally, its links to social unrest running the gamut from ethnic conflict and secessionist movements to terrorism-prone insurgencies after World War II, not only in Europe but also in the former colonial areas. (Ironically, it fell out of favor morally and ideologically in Europe even as it was coming into its own in the Middle East, Africa, and Asia.) But there is another side to nationalism, one that is now only dimly perceived by the public and seldom mentioned by politicians, journalists and other close observers. As Professor David Calleo has written,

> Nationalism might more properly be defined in its normal healthy, rather than occasionally diseased, form. It is [a] theory of the state which holds that consensus can be achieved successfully only within the community of identity established by a *national* culture.... The

> nationalist [sought]...a degree of common identity and civic spirit that would rally the contentious elements of society towards rational cooperation within [a] generally accepted constitutional framework.[3]

Moreover, as Calleo notes, "modern democracy has almost never been established outside the context of a national state...."[4]

Thus, the importance of nationalism in modern European history can be exaggerated only with difficulty, but its positive side is easily overlooked or denigrated. Indeed, nation-building on the Continent was the "major preoccupation" of old and new states alike in the nineteenth century.[5] This point is a key to understanding the paradox of contemporary Europe – integrating into a single economy while simultaneously sub-dividing into a larger number of sovereign states than ever before in its history.

Lingering nationalism is still ubiquitous at the start of the twenty-first century, but that does not necessarily mean that a politically united Europe is impossible. European history stands as testimony to this startling truth: if something can be imagined it can be accomplished – for better or worse – given the right set of circumstances. The rise of totalitarian tyrannies in Stalin's Russia and Hitler's Germany in the first half of the twentieth century proved the negative; the emergence of the European "communities" in the second half of the twentieth century culminating in the recent birth of the European Union proves the positive.

Europe's greatest thinkers have imagined Europe as a single political unit at least since the time of the Roman Empire; in the modern era, ideas on the unity of Europe can be traced back to the fourteenth century, to Dante and Pierre DuBois, counselor to Philip the Fair.[6] Thereafter, the list of luminaries favoring a united Europe would grow through the centuries – King George Podiebrad of Bohemia, Emeric Cruce, the Duc de Sully, Comenius, William Penn, the Abbe de Saint Pierre, Count Henri de Saint-Simon, Jeremy Bentham, Victor Hugo, P-J. Proudhon, to name but a few.[7]

The two "world wars" gave the European movement new impetus and, during the second of these, a sense of urgency.[8] In the darkest days of 1940, Winston Churchill actually offered to merge the British and French governments![9] At the end of the war, Churchill and de Gaulle both embraced the idea of confederation, but by this time ardent federalists had stolen a march on the politicians.

In 1944, representatives from nine European countries met in secret at a villa in Geneva, Switzerland, to make common cause against Hitler's Germany. It was imperative, they admonished, "to supersede the dogma of absolute state sovereignty by joining together in a single federal organization."[10] Noting ruefully "in the space of a single generation Europe has been the epicenter of two world conflicts due primarily to the existence of thirty sovereign states on this continent," they declared: "This anarchy must be ended by the creation of a federal Union among the peoples of Europe."[11]

The impetus for a united Europe did not end in 1945 when the guns finally fell silent. On the contrary, across the Continent "a multitude of movements, groups, associations and leagues committed to the idea of federation" sprang up. A meeting at Montreux (Switzerland) in 1947 led to the convening of the *Congress of Europe* at The Hague (the Netherlands) in the spring of 1948 – the beginning of the European project now known as the European Union.[12] As this essay underscores, however, it is a project that, for all its remarkable achievements, remains far from completion. Moreover, despite the formidable obstacles that have had to be overcome, it is fair to say that what has been accomplished up to now, is the easy part, relatively speaking. The hard part – political amalgamation – remains a distant goal, one that is not shared by all Europeans or viewed in the same way even by those who do.[13]

What Europeans Share

What *do* Europeans have in common? Europe's rich heritage in philosophy, science and the fine arts is a colorful tapestry of contributions from all the nations huddled together on that small "continent".[*] No single country can claim to have created European civilization. Nor is demographic or geographic size a reliable guide to

---

[*] According to a famous description by Paul Valéry, Europe is "a kind of promontory of the ancient continent, a western appendix of Asia" rather than a continent apart. Similarly, the *Georgraphie universelle* of Mantelle and Brun, published in Paris in 1816, refers to Europe as "This narrow peninsula, which appears on the map as no more than an appendix of Asia...." Quoted in Denis de Rougemont, *The Meaning of Europe* (New York: Stein and Day, 1965, pp. 13-14.

the relative value of each nation's contribution in a given field. For example, the Czech contribution to Europe's treasury of classical music far exceeds that nation's diminutive size, and the Dutch have produced a similar disproportion of great artists. Indeed, calling something a "Rembrandt" is a universal form of flattery, and not only in aesthetic matters.

Europe's creativity and dynamism is apparent in the material world of industry and technology, as well.[14] It was, of course, Europe that launched the Industrial Age in the eighteenth century. Before that, advances in maritime and military technology propelled Europe into the era of the so-called Great Discoveries that preceded the drive to colonize most of the non-European world.[15] In the first half of the twentieth century, the very same dynamism revealed its dark side in catastrophic wars and totalitarian revolutions.

Europeans also share a common religious tradition and political history replete with similar (if not identical) institutions, from papacy to monarchy. But kings divided Europe more successfully than popes united it. In the final analysis, politics trumps religion in Europe. For obvious reasons, Europe's kings cultivated one other value that today's Europeans share (in a paradoxical way): nationalism. The problem, of course, is that there is a separate brand of nationalism for every nation in Europe.

Nationalism was once indispensable to kings facing the challenge of building modern states from the ground up, so to speak. Today, however, it is the major obstacle to the reconstitution of Europe as a single super-state, federal or otherwise. Does this mean that a federation of European states is out of the question? Not necessarily. What it *does* mean is that any political union will probably have to wait until a new European political culture and consciousness – in effect, a new European *nation* – is fully formed.

For centuries the focus of Europe's visionary unifiers was on the desired *product*. After World War II, however, a new breed of "Eurocrats" gained the ascendancy and shifted attention decisively toward the *process*.

Theoretically, the only two schemes that make any sense in the European context are a confederation or a federation. The idea of confederation has attracted many adherents over the centuries. As recently as the 1960s, French President Charles de Gaulle tried unsuccessfully to sell such a plan to France's Common Market partners.[16]

European federalists often distrust executive power, be it wielded by kings or presidents (modern-day kings). According to one scholar, the dream of a unified Europe "is powered not only by the drive to build Europe, but by the desire to propose a substitute for that form of presidential government which has come increasingly to predominate within the modern national state."[17] They take a dim view of "power politics" in general and typically emphasize economic relationships rather than military might. As technocrats by temperament and training, they are also far more comfortable dealing with domestic problems than international conflict.[18]

This "technocratic ideal" is vitally important to understanding the process that is taking place in Europe at present. Its basic tenet is "that many of the problems that presently plague humankind could be solved if only decisions could be left to impartial, scientifically trained experts whose efforts were not continually distorted by the emotional and hasty generalizations of mass politics."[19] In the eyes of the Eurocrats, presidents typically appeal to "mass politics" in order to circumvent or checkmate a recalcitrant legislature or simply to whip up patriotism in times of crisis. Europeans did not survive centuries of autocratic rule and, more recently, decades of totalitarian tyranny only to give supreme power to a popularly elected "king."

To describe this attitude is to suggest the wide gap between America's political traditions and Europe's emerging political culture. The latter is not based on a formal ideology but rather on an informal set of core values embraced in varying degrees by most Europeans depending on the specific value and the issues associated with it.

In the following sections I elucidate these core values and pinpoints some sources of tension within and between them. I also examine how abstract values are expressed in the concrete issues and controversies that animate European politics today. Throughout, I give special emphasis to the challenges posed by the historic expansion of the EU to include many former communist states in Eastern Europe.

A Culture of Liberty

At the dawn of the twentieth century, most Europeans had still never voted in a meaningful election and, with few exceptions, existing constitutions did little to limit royal powers or protect individual rights. Indeed, the very idea of *civil* society as a web of relationships among citizens independent of the state had not yet taken root.

How Europe has changed! Following the collapse of communist rule, a wave of democracy rolled across the eastern flank of the Continent in the 1990s. Today, even Russia, long a synonym for political oppression, is ruled by a popularly elected president whose powers – however broad – are limited by a new constitution and functioning legislature. In Europe, the triumph of the West was, above all, the triumph of liberal democracy.

It is difficult to exaggerate the importance of this development. What divided Europe, politically and ideology, since the French Revolution was not only nationalism but also the idea of liberty. This subversive idea was the antithesis of absolute monarchy in the nineteenth century and of totalitarianism in the twentieth century. The twenty-first century promises to be utterly different in this all-important respect.

Europeans of all nationalities have suffered in one way or another from the actions of tyrants; in modern Europe, oppression and aggression are both closely related to the absence of constitutional constraints on power. Thus, Europeans understand even better than most Americans that freedom and security are indivisible. Now that the vast majority of Europe's peoples have won the right to vote, to dissent and, if all else fails, to emigrate, it is highly unlikely that any of them will give up these rights willingly. It is fair to say, therefore, that Europe's Age of Liberty, after two centuries in the offing, has finally dawned.

The experience of liberty may be relatively new to some 360 million Europeans who lived on the "wrong side" of the Iron Curtain during the Cold War (1945-1989), but the idea itself is definitely not.[†]

[†] The number of Europeans who did not experience democracy directly prior to the 1990s is roughly equal to the number who did. Approximately 360 million people inhabit the former communist countries of Eastern Europe and the Balkans; the total population of the 15 members of the European Union in the 1990s was about 375 million, but that number includes some 17

The "pedigree" and geographical proximity of this idea means that democracy had a head start in Eastern Europe in the 1990s in comparison with Africa, the Middle East and Asia. Hungarians may not have experienced constitutional democracy until the 1990s, but they have long known about it (and occasionally fought for it).‡

As we will see, freedom in the context of liberal democracy is about the only political value that does not divide Europeans today. Other values, even those that most Europeans hold dear, cause divisions based on nation, social class or generation. This broad embrace of liberty, then, is a key element in the new European political culture, one that gives a measure of cohesion to an otherwise highly contentious community of nation-states. Ironically, critics of the European Union have often decried what they call a "democratic deficit" – namely, the absence of any direct connection between voters and decision-making institutions or processes within the EU.[20]

The Expectation of Prosperity

Europeans associate liberty with *prosperity*. Significantly, only states that are stable democracies with open societies and market economies are considered for membership in the European Union. The decision to admit 10 new members in 2004 attests to the continuing importance of these criteria, as well as the widespread belief that membership in the EU is the best guarantee of a prosperous future.

---

million former East Germans who belong on the other side of the "line" in this comparison. The only noteworthy exception is Czechoslovakia, which functioned as a full-blown parliamentary democracy between the two world wars.

‡ Witness the Hungarian Revolution of 1956 when a spontaneous popular uprising would have swept away communist rule but for a brutal Soviet intervention.

Table 1.0
GNP in the European Union:
A Country Comparison

Country	GNP (billions $)	Per Capita GNP (thousands $)	Population
Austria	217	26,830	8,080,000
Belgium	259	25,380	10,200,000
Denmark	175	33,040	5,300,000
Finland	125	24,280	5,153,000
France	1,465	24,210	58,847,000
Germany	2,180	26,570	82,047,000
Greece	123	11,740	10,515,000
Ireland	69	18,710	3.705,000
Italy	1,157	20,090	57,589,000
Luxembourg	19	45,100	427,000
Netherlands	389	24,780	15,698,000
Portugal	106	10,670	9,968,000
Spain	555	14,100	39,371,000
Sweden	1,264	19,848	8,852,000
UK	1,264	21,410	59,055,000

Total EU GNP = $8.33 trillion

Source: *The World Bank Atlas 2000*, pp. 24-25 & 42-43.

Of course, people everywhere desire prosperity and Europeans are no different, except that, like Americans, they have come to *expect* it. Income disparities among social classes, age groups, nations and regions in Europe can cause envy and inevitably give rise to clashes of interest that undermine efforts to broaden and deepen economic integration.

Significant disparities in wealth and living standards in Western Europe still exist. These disparities give rise to clashes of interest and complicate the political process within the EU. In the Europe of the Fifteen, for example, Portugal, Greek, Spain and Ireland were still relatively poor in the late 1990s by comparison with the other 11 members. Nor does wealth exclusively correlate with size: Lilliputian

Luxembourg and diminutive Denmark are the wealthiest countries in the EU. (See Table 1.0)

The relative position of national economies does not change over night and it often happens that the rich get richer and the poor stay poor. Historically, the dynamism of the European Union and the sheer size of its market have meant that new members get a boost upon entry, but membership in the EU can also be a double-edged sword because domestic producers often find it daunting to compete on a playing field that is home to so many world-class multinational corporations. Gaining ground in this competitive arena is not easy, as a snapshot of the EU in 2003 reveals (see Table 1.1).

Table 1.1
The Rich and Not-So-Rich:
Selected EU Countries in 2003

	GDP (billion $)	GDP per capita	GDP growth	Inflation
Denmark	$210	$39,050	2.4%	2.0%
Sweden	$292	$32,800	2.5%	1.9%
Finland	$163	$31,090	2.9%	1.5%
UK	$1,771	$29,360	2.1%	1.2%
Austria	$240	$29,310	2.2%	1.6%
Germany	$2,392	$29,210	2.0%	1.4%
France	$1,677	$27,890	2.1%	1.5%
Italy	$1,422	$24,700	2.6%	2.2%
Spain	$763	$18,710	2.8%	2.6%
Greece	$160	$15,060	3.7%	3.3%
Portugal	$142	$14,070	1.1%	3.0%

Source: The World in 2003, *The Economist*, pp. 93-94.

Nonetheless, even the poorest EU members are far richer than the former communist states; Slovenia, the richest, had a per capita GNP slightly lower than that of Portugal in the late 1990s. Eastern Europe as a whole remains far behind the EU countries by any standard of comparison (see Table 1.2). Next to Slovenia, the Czech Republic is the richest country in Eastern Europe, but it still lags far behind "poor" Portugal in GDP per capita. The Ukraine, the second largest East

European state, remains abysmally poor by EU standards with no prospect of good government or an economic turnaround any time soon. Poland's GDP was bigger than that of Portugal or Greece, the poorest EU members prior to 2004, but its per capita GDP was only about one-third as much. Overall, the per capita gross domestic product of the 10 expansion countries 2001 (the most recent EU figures available) was about $5,500 compared to $23,000 for the 15 already in the "club".[21]

The list of new members set to join that club in 2004 encompasses eight former communist states, plus Cyprus and Malta. Together with these two little island republics, the addition of Poland, Hungary, Slovenia, Slovakia, the Czech Republic and the three Baltic states (Latvia, Lithuania and Estonia) will increase the EU population by 20 percent (or 75 million people), its territory by 25 percent, but its gross domestic product by only about 5 percent.[22]

Table 1.2
Four at the Core:
Selected Accession States in 2003

	GDP (billion $)	GDP per capita	GDP growth	Inflation
Czech Republic	$91	$8,880	4.0%	1.9%
Hungary	$77	$7,690	4.3%	5.3%
Poland	$198	$5,120	2.9%	3.3%
Slovakia	$27	$4,900	4.2%	5.7%

Source: The World in 2003, *The Economist*, p. 95.

In 1998, the combined GDP of the EU's 15 members was over $8.3 trillion (it had risen to over $9 trillion by 2003). The combined GDP of the 10 new members was only about $322 *billion* – considerably smaller than that of the Netherlands alone. Except for Malta, Cyprus and Slovenia, the accession states have a dismal GDP per head of between 16 percent and 26 percent of the EU average. As a consequence, EU development funds will "eventually flow east rather than south."[23] Not surprisingly, the Portuguese are far less enthusiastic about the prospect of EU expansion than voters in several other small EU states.[24]

A Cherished Diversity

Is it possible to be for economic integration and against moves to strengthen the European Union? Perhaps the best answer to this question is found in the writings, speeches and policies of General Charles de Gaulle, the founder of France's Fifth Republic and its first president. That de Gaulle placed an indelible mark on French politics is well known. What is less often remembered is that he also played a major role in the shaping of modern Europe. Indeed, during the first decade after the signing of the Rome Treaty (1958) that launched the Common Market nobody was more assertive in promoting a particular vision of Europe than President de Gaulle.

De Gaulle is best remembered as a staunch nationalist. In the mid-1960s, he was the only major political leader in Europe who spoke out in praise of nationalism.[25] But he was by no means a voice in the wilderness. As one close observer wrote, "he seems sufficiently formidable to freeze the movement towards European federal unity, and, if he lives long enough, to wreck it."[26] In fact, De Gaulle did not live long enough to wreck "the movement towards European federal unity," but he did slow it down and by providing an alternative vision of Europe he posed a challenge to all who dreamt of a Europe without nation-states or "old-fashioned" nationalism.

De Gaulle was vehemently opposed to supranationalism. He did not think nationalism was old-fashioned or outmoded. Quite the contrary: he argued compellingly that there is no substitute in the modern world for the nation-state as an instrument of political authority or as an effective actor in the arena of international politics.

But de Gaulle was no war-mongering reactionary. He favored the creation of a European confederation based on a Franco-German entente that would institutionalize cooperative ties and coordinate economic policies among existing national governments.[27] His plan, in other words, was to leave the sovereignty of states in tact while facilitating trade and commerce and building trust at the grass roots level. To have an effective state, de Gaulle believed, it is necessary, above all, to have a "moral entity sufficiently living, established and recognized to obtain the congenital loyalty of its subjects…and, if it should happen, that millions of men would be willing to die for it."[28]

De Gaulle, the professional soldier, was especially scornful of the federalists' pet project in the early 1950s – namely the creation of a European Defense Community. It would not be a European Army, he asserted, but merely "the army called European" probably under the command of an American![29]

> At the base of the defense of peoples, there are the peoples themselves. This profound force cannot be replaced by technique. Wars are not fought simply by Pentagons, by GHQs, by Shapes, or NATOs. Wars are fought with the blood and souls of men. Neither European nor Atlantic defense can be built except on the base of realities and those realities are national. There are no others, except, of course, in the formularies of politicians." [30]

Following De Gaulle's personal campaign against the European army, which was defeated in the French National Assembly in 1954, he withdrew from politics to write his *Memoirs*.

When de Gaulle returned in 1958, it was not for the purpose of losing the nation he had just rescued in a nebulous Europe. Nonetheless, de Gaulle never abandoned his commitment to European unity. But de Gaulle talked about unity it was in the context of the real Europe, not the Europe of the federalists' dreams. In the real Europe, states were "very different from one another, each has its own spirit, its own history, its own language, its own misfortunes, glories and ambitions." They alone "have the right to order and the authority to act." To imagine otherwise – "this is a dream."

As noted above, De Gaulle's gave his proposal for a European confederation concrete expression in the so-called Fouchet Plan in 1961 (see above). One of the plans key features was a de Gaulle trademark: it called for a popular referendum in the member states to legitimate the whole enterprise. De Gaulle's fondness for this device reminiscent of Napoleon Bonaparte was controversial and certainly one of the reasons why the Fouchet Plan failed to win the approval of the other Common Market states.

At this point, the reader may be asking: Why dwell on an idea put forward so long ago that failed? The question is fair enough, but the

The European Union Today

answer is surprisingly simple. De Gaulle was obviously out of step with many of Europe's politicians and intellectuals in the 1960s, but time has proven he was essentially correct in his assessment. More than four decades after the Fouchet Plan failed, the dream of a European federation remains just that – a dream. For all Europe's success in economic integration (always high on de Gaulle's list of desirable outcomes), the European Union has *at best* made only modest and faltering progress toward political federation.

Let us "fast forward" now to 2003. The EU was preparing to bring ten new members (75 million people) under the big tent in the next year. Ironically, the circus analogy would have struck many Europeans, including many of the 105 delegates to the Convention on the Future of Europe, as entirely appropriate. After 16 months of debate and deliberation, the Convention had finally produced a draft of what it hoped would eventually become Europe's first constitution. A reporter for *The New York Times* summed it up this way: "The process has been awkward and unpredictable, ambitious and timid, as delegates from the 15 member nations of the European Union and the 10 that are to join next year fight to protect their countries' national interests even as they agree to cede bits of sovereignty."[31] Similarly, one of two vice presidents of the convention expressed dissatisfaction with the result, complaining:

> Too many member states are defending themselves instead of sharing power at the European level to make things to make things better. It's each state beyond the constitution. That's why I'm not even sure we are entitled to call it a constitution. [32]

The "process" itself speaks volumes: as a showcase of Europe's deep-rooted cultural and political diversity, it would have come as no surprise to Charles de Gaulle. But the process did not end in Brussels. The next step involved formal presentation of the draft at a summit meeting of the EU heads of state in Greece, followed by an intergovernmental review giving each member state one last chance to demand changes. Finally, each national parliament – including those of the 10 new members – must ratify the document before it comes into force. Some countries (Ireland and Denmark, for example) have a constitutional rule that requires a national referendum for approval of any new step of this kind.

The issues that surfaced at the EU constitution-drafting convention in Brussels vividly illustrate the sense in which political and cultural diversity remains a vibrant fact of life in contemporary Europe. As the American founders discovered at the Philadelphia Convention, federalism juxtaposes the interests of big and small states in the starkest form. Hence, at Brussels, France and other big states favored a strong president from a large country – "an idea that is anathema to the smaller states."

The chairman of the convention, former French President Giscard d'Estaing, attacked the existing principle that each member state is entitled to one European Commissioner and one vote: "His aides point out that in an enlarged EU of 25 countries, the seven smallest ones representing a paltry 1.5 percent of the EU's GDP will have more voting weight in the European Commission than the six largest countries with 82 percent of the Union's GDP."[33] He also proposed making seats in the European Parliament more proportional to population and extending the tenure in office of the EU president to as much as 5 years.[34] (Under the existing system the presidency rotates among all the member-states every six months.)

From a geopolitical perspective, Europe is a region of small nations historically dominated by a few big ones. The great majority of EU member-states – 19 out of 25 after 2004 – will be small states with a strong tendency to weigh matters of national interest on the same scale. The average size of the 199 small states is only about 5 million, ranging from 15.7 million (the Netherlands) to a mere 377,000 (Malta). The total population of the 19 is only about 20 percent larger than that of Germany.

Not surprisingly, the small states within the EU generally oppose attempts by big states like France to gain political advantage or special treatment based on population size. Thus, they insist on retaining the principle of equality in the EU Commission. By the same token, the stand taken on key policy issues by two middle-sized states, Spain and Poland, could become decisively important in the future because these two member-states, each with a population of slightly under 40 million, are not as big as Germany, France, Italy and Great Britain nor as small as the others. Spain has fought against changing the EU's majority voting rules that "give it power disproportionate to its population" (and almost equal to that of Germany even though Germans outnumber Spaniards by two to one).[35]

Some EU members remain deeply skeptical about any steps toward political federation. The British government, for example, insists on the right of any member to veto decisions on foreign policy and taxation – two areas that cut to the very core of national sovereignty. Germany, on the other hand, has obvious historical reasons for seeking to allay its neighbors' fears and no reason to fear a federation in which it would be the biggest constituent part.[36]

These differences are merely illustrative: a catalogue of national concerns would be just that – a catalogue the size of a phone book. Of course not all the contentious issues at the Brussels convention were tied to the big state-small state split. Some issues go to the very heart of democracy itself. For example, decision-making within the EU is not transparent even to members of the European Parliament (much less the public).[37] But for avid Eurocrats and supranationalists there is a democratic dilemma that confounds benign intentions: making decisions more transparent will further complicate an already cumbersome process. Imagine having French farmers protesting over agricultural policy set in Brussels! How would Paris deal with that kind of a predicament?

De Gaulle recognized that for a European super-state to exist there would have to be a leader (or leaders) capable of inspiring loyalty in the hearts of Europeans of every nationality – a super-nation. The delegates at Brussels bowed to de Gaulle's memory, so to speak, by agreeing to create a single foreign minister – that is easier said than done, of course, but if it happens it will be a significant step in the direction of a common European foreign policy.

That said, however, what good is a European foreign policy without a European army? Simply to ask the question is to suggest how far Europe is from anything resembling a self-sufficient political union – one, that is, capable of standing on its own militarily and standing up to the United States in disputes over the use of force (such as the invasion of Iraq in 2003). The new European constitution talks vaguely of "structured cooperation" in the realm of defense, but goes no further. It does not pledge member states to commit resources to a European army and does not dare to mention the possibility of creating a European nuclear deterrent or seeking a seat at the United Nations. The latter would probably require the United Kingdom and France to give up the seats they hold as permanent members of the Security Council.

Much to the chagrin of the "federalists" and supranationalists, Europe will continue to have two presidents under the prospective constitution. One president heads the Council of the European Union while the other heads the European Commission (see Thomas Magstadt, *Nations and Governments*, pages 165-172.) Of course, neither president is directly elected and neither, therefore, has any kind of European mandate. Whether an "animal with two heads" can survive is not really the question.[38] The question is whether an animal with two heads can decide to go in one direction or the other. A single Europe paralyzed by indecision – a kind of inept giant – is almost certainly not what most Europeans want or would enthusiastically support.

To end this brief discussion of Europe's national diversity with an exclamation point, the Brussels constitution would be published in 11 languages in 2003 and no fewer than 21 languages the next year with the accession of 10 new members. Even the Czechs and the Slovaks who were part of a single state (Czechoslovakia) for most of the twentieth century would require two separate languages. It would probably be enough to make even the redoubtable Charles de Gaulle smile just a little.

A Desire for Unity

So far the reader has found out that Europe is a region of great economic, cultural and linguistic diversity in which nationalism has not been extinguished by any stretch of the imagination, despite a half-century of progress toward a full economic integration over an ever-larger area. If that is the case, why all the talk about European unity? Is it wishful thinking or, worse, a smokescreen to hide the underlying reality of a fragmented and quarrelsome region where the next war is just around the corner?

Neither. Anyone who fails to see how far Europe has moved away from its war-prone past is blind to the sweeping changes that are transforming the Continent. Simply put, the Europe of today is a very different place from the Europe of a half-century ago when the European Coal and Steel Community (ECSC) – the first small step toward a single economy – came into being. Europe has not had the luxury of following a well-worn path. Rather, it has had to blaze a trail from the old European "war system" to the new Europe in which war has virtually disappeared as an instrument of foreign policy. The fact that getting from the old to the new Europe meant passing through a protracted period when the Continent was politically and economically divided by an "iron curtain" makes the achievements that culminated in the Europe of the 25 all the more remarkable.

As we noted earlier, Europeans proudly share a common heritage, one that is unique to West. (Readers are encouraged to review the material in Chapter 3 of *Nations and Governments*, especially pages 79-93.) We will not repeat what has already been said elsewhere, but it is important to note that Europe's ethnic and linguistic differences are counter-balanced by religious and artistic commonalities. The latter have not precluded national rivalries and inter-state wars, but it is equally true that the former have not drowned out voices calling for European unity since as far back as the Middle Ages. It was only after the catastrophe of World War II, however, that Europeans began taking the concrete steps that have made this desire for unity without uniformity more than wishful thinking. The result is plain to see: the European Union in 2004 will have a population of 450 million citizens, exceeded in sheer mass only by China and India, and an economy of more than $9 trillion, nearly equal to that of the United States.

For the general public, the desire for unity in the context of European history is, above all, a desire for peace. This point can hardly be exaggerated, but it is easily overlooked now that the last great European war for the vast majority of EU citizens exists only in history books. In 1952, the European Coal and Steel Community (ECSC) brought together six countries – France, Germany, Belgium, the Netherlands, Luxembourg, and Italy – that had been enemies in World War II. In addition to the economic rationale of coordinating investment in two basic industries, the ECSC was intended "to reduce the risk of war between historic enemies by integrating industries essential for war production."[39] The fundamental importance of energy and iron products in the creation of national military capabilities is well documented in scholarly literature on international politics and clearly illustrated by modern European history.[40] In sum, for Europeans who had been in the middle of the maelstrom in both world wars to take this dramatic step in the early 1950s was, above all, an attempt to avert the worst consequence of disunity, namely another major war.

Stressing the strong desire for peace as a motive force in post-war European politics is not to diminish the importance of prosperity as a reason for greater unity. Europeans see a logical three-way connection between peace and prosperity, prosperity and unity, and unity and peace. The "functionalists" who worked so hard to establish the original European communities in the 1950s believed that this dynamic could be best by kick-started by promoting economic integration.[41]

Is it true? Does unity (integration) promote prosperity or were European functionalists making a leap of faith that has no basis in reality? It is easy to demonstrate that prosperity in Europe does correlate positively with economic integration, but a correlation does not necessarily prove cause and effect. There is no way of knowing, for example, whether Portugal would have a significantly lower standard of living today if it had not joined the EU in 1986 or if it would be significantly higher had Portugal joined in 1958. At the same time, some European countries that do not belong to the EU are more prosperous that do. Norway, for example, which does not belong to the EU, is Europe's richest country. It had a per capita GDP of $48,710 in 2003. Sweden, Norway's next-door neighbor and a member of the EU since 1995, has a much lower per capita GDP (about $32,800). Similarly, Switzerland would be the wealthiest country in the EU (except for tiny Luxembourg) if it belonged but has chosen to stay out. Denmark, which has chosen not to be a part of the Euro zone, ranks right behind Switzerland on the roster of Europe's richest countries.

Nonetheless, there is a widespread *belief* that membership in the EU is a ticket on the gravy train. Economists agree that large open markets encourage efficiency through competition and economies of scale, a more rational allocation of resources (including both labor and capital), comparative advantage, and the like. Logic and evidence are two different things, but the evidence *does* suggest that economic integration has promoted growth and dynamism in Europe even though it is equally clear that you can be rich and not belong to the "club."

The EU itself is a monument to the fact that political elites in Europe place a high premium on unity. Major political parties sometimes appeal to voters to reject certain policies under consideration in Brussels but rarely, if ever, advocate withdrawing from the EU or, in the case of new applicants, not joining.[42] The British, for example, have always been more skeptical of federal schemes and more reluctant to relinquish sovereignty over key areas of national policy than many of the other member states, but neither of the two major parties has ever advocated getting out of the EU. Like the British, Denmark, Sweden, and Greece opted to stay out of the Euro zone when it was launched in 1999, but Greece joined in 2001 and Sweden was expected to join following a national referendum on the question in 2003.

Political elites frequently have different ideas on the major issues of the day than the general public. What politicians and bureaucrats cook up is not always in step with public opinion. This observation would seem to apply with special force to a kind of proto-state like the EU.[43] By "proto-state" I mean that the EU is somewhat more than an international organization of sovereign states but much less than a sovereign state in its own right. Given the fact there is little direct connection between European citizens and the institutions European Union, it would be somewhat surprising if ordinary people from countries as different as Portugal and Poland or France and Finland expressed patriotic feelings toward the EU.

As we have seen, the trappings of the EU are democratic, but actual decision- making processes within the EU are neither democratic nor transparent. If the process had made more democratic, however, it would probably have slowed the pace of progress toward closer economic integration and perhaps even have blocked it altogether. This "democratic dilemma" makes it all the more remarkable that, by and large, Europeans express strong support for the EU, both in public opinion polls and in the voting booth. Citizens of the original six members are generally more supportive than citizens of Great Britain and Denmark. Thus, Danish voters said "no" to joining the EU and the UK's popular Prime Minister Tony Blair in 2003 reaffirmed London's intention to stay out of the Euro zone for the time being, as well.[44]

Although public support for the EU varies from country to country, a solid majority expresses overall support everywhere. In 2000, only a tiny fraction of the electorate in Ireland, Luxembourg, the Netherlands, and Spain expressed strong negative feelings for the EU. That percentage was quite a bit higher in Austria and Sweden, as well as Denmark and the UK, but only in Sweden was it above 25 percent.[45] In the original Big Three (France, Germany and Italy), on the other hand, overwhelming majorities express support for the EU.[46]

A further indication of popular support for the EU (and thus for European unity) in 2003 was the overwhelming "yes" vote in national referenda in Eastern Europe. In Poland, for example, 77 percent voted in favor of joining the EU.[47] Voters in the Czech Republic also strongly endorsed the accession, as they had earlier in Lithuania, Slovakia, and Hungary.[48] All early indications were that voters in Estonia and Latvia would follow suit later in the year.

To sum up, Europeans are akin to a quarrelsome "family" with a history of fratricidal warfare who have learned "the hard way" that they have a lot to gain by getting along together – and too much to lose not to. At the same time, Europeans – no less than Americans and Canadians, for example – prefer to speak the national language and exhibit a robust "love of one's own" in architecture, music, manners, sports, food, and the like. In short, the desire for unity co-exists, at times uneasily, with the reality of diversity. Finally, what makes continued expansion of the EU community possible – and even inevitable – is that Europeans from the Atlantic to the Urals are governed more or less democratically; that they want freedom, peace and prosperity; and that they associate all three with the movement toward a united Europe.

Nonetheless, the road ahead is bumpy, at best. In the final analysis, the political future of Europe hinges on whether or not Europeans will eventually come to respect and trust Brussels as much (or more than) they trust their own national governments.

Ambivalence Toward EU Authority

How much real authority to give the EU is the opposite side of the question: How much authority can member-states cede without losing the very sovereignty that they have so often fought so ferociously to protect. In theory, there seems to be no way solution to this problem. The contradiction between the desire for unity and the near-reverence for sovereignty appear to be on a collision course. The EU has avoided a crack-up only by avoiding a showdown on certain key questions; by allowing member-states to opt out of certain arrangements; and, finally, by carefully balancing the danger of trying to go too fast against the hazards of going too slow.[49]

One secret to the success of the EU so far, like that of Europe in a larger historic sense, is it dynamism. Hence, the European communities have expanded no fewer than five times in less than 50 years. Then, too, member-states have entered into a series of treaties aimed at strengthening and tightening the ties that bind them.[50] (See Box 4.4, "Tightening the Knot: The Treaties of Europe's Union," in Thomas Magstadt, *Nations and Governments*, p. 171.) Since the decision to create a single market in 1985, the balance between national and European legislation has shifted dramatically, according to many close observers. In 2003, the London-based *Economist* canvassed the major Brussels institutions and embassies and reported: "…of those prepared to offer a number, all reckoned that EU legislation now accounts for more than 50 percent of new laws."[51]

But despite this rapid growth in EU legislation related to the internal market there are still major areas of national policy that remain largely off-limits to the EU Commission and the European Parliament:

> The EU may account for more than half of all legislation across the Union, but it tends to deal with the boring stuff. The issues that get people marching in the street – pensions, welfare benefits, education – are still largely run at a national level, although the EU is beginning to nibble at the edges.[52]

Perhaps the most revealing single statistic about the difference between rapid progress on the internal market and the slow pace of political power transfers from national capitals to Brussels is the relative size of the EU budget. The EU budget was a paltry 1 percent of its members' total GDP in 2002-2003; by comparison, the federal budget in United States was about 24 percent of GDP.[53] Until (or unless) the European Union wins the right to levy taxes, all talk of a federal Europe in the foreseeable future will be indicative of either wishful thinking or paranoia.

In early 2002, the EU embarked one of its most ambitious projects to date: a constitution-drafting convention. Hitherto, treaties have framed the EU's structures and defined its powers, beginning with the Treaty of Rome of 1958 and culminating in the Treaty of Amsterdam in 1997. That the constitution hammered out in Brussels and tentatively endorsed at a European Union summit in Greece by the 15 member states in June 2003 is also a *treaty* is a point of enormous symbolic and practical importance. The new EU constitution will not go into effect until it has been duly ratified by each and every one of the individual member states (including the 10 new members) as prescribed in their respective national constitutions. In other words, sovereignty still clearly rests with the member-states. So unassailable is this principle that even a tiny member-state like Luxembourg (population: 427,000) or Malta (population: 377,000) can, theoretically, prevent the constitution of the new EU (population: 450 million) from going into effect!

Deference to the issue of sovereignty is clearly apparent in the disproportionate power of small states within the EU scheme of things (see Table 1.3). As noted earlier, every member state is entitled to at least one Commissioner and even the largest states get no more than two Commissioners. The Commission decides by majority vote what policy measures to propose to the Council of Ministers or the European Parliament. Thus, between 1995-2004 the 10 smallest member states carried the same voting weight in the Commission as the five largest states. The situation in the Council of Ministers was not much different. There, Spain was the holder of the balance of power: if Spain joined the small states they had an absolute majority of 47 votes to 40 votes for the big states; if Spain voted with the big states, the balance shifted 48 to 39 against the small states. Although voting in the Council of Ministers probably does not strictly break down along big state-small state lines as a rule, nonetheless the decision-making "arithmetic" says a lot about the importance of sovereignty.

Until 1985 all decisions taken by the Council of Ministers required unanimity, which meant that every member-state could theoretically exercise a veto over every issue. In 1987 the EU ratified the Single European Act the EU, which amended the Treaty of Rome and made qualified majority voting QMV) the rule for most legislation aimed at creating a single internal market. (Qualified majority voting requires broader approval than simple majority voting.) The significance of this decision transcended the question of procedural. By abolishing the unanimity rule in one policy area it established the principle that state sovereignty does not always trump EU authority. At the same time, the EU moved cautiously, retain the requirement for unanimity on such sensitive single-market issues as taxes, border controls, immigration, and labor-management relations.

During the 1990s, the principle of QMV decision-making in the Council of Ministers remained more or less frozen in place, despite the adoption of two important new treaties during that decade that expedited EU enlargement and established the Economic and Monetary Union (EMU). The Treaty of Amsterdam (1997) modified arrangements agreed upon at Maastricht five years earlier whereby the Council of Ministers and the European Parliament would share legislative powers in certain areas (a procedure the EU calls "codecision"). The net effect of the codecision procedure is to give the European Parliament the appearance of a real legislative function while changing the substance of the EU legislative process only at the margins.

The Maastricht and Amsterdam Treaties divided the EU into three "pillars" – the European Community (the internal market), the Common Foreign and Security Policy and Justice and Home Affairs. These treaties did little to fill the void created by the absence of a mechanism for formulating and articulating common EU foreign and defense policies. The lack of a common foreign and defense policy was evident in the Bosnian crisis in the mid-1990s and Iraq invasion in 2003. In the latter case, four of the five EU biggest states lined up on opposite sides – the UK and Spain strongly backed the US decision to invade, while France and Germany wanted to give the UN more time to resolve the dispute (over weapons inspections) peacefully.

There has been a little more movement toward federalization in the realm of the third pillar – Justice and Home Affairs.[54] This pillar involves issues related to law enforcement, including asylum, immigration, fugitive criminals, terrorism, and drugs. In general, it is up to the interior ministers of the member-states to coordinate national policies in these areas. National laws still operate but the Council of Ministers can adopt conventions that define new rules and procedures for the EU as a whole by a qualified majority vote in some instances. Theoretically, functions can be shifted from the third pillar to the first pillar (the EC) by a unanimous vote in the Council but practically nothing of consequence has changed. By and large, national police, investigative bodies, intelligence services, and criminal courts continue to operate under procedural rules and criminal codes set at the national level, not in Brussels.

The terrorist attacks on the World Trade Center and the Pentagon on September 11, 2001, had law-enforcement repercussions in Europe as well as the United States. There was a new sense of urgency about the need for greater coordination among national police and intelligence services in the war on terrorism. President George W. Bush threw down the gauntlet famously declaring, "You are either with the us or with the terrorists." This challenge (like the terrorist threat itself) conveniently handed European federalists a case for accelerating the effort to expand the EU's law-enforcement powers as well as seek closer coordination of police and intelligence functions in Brussels.[55] Hence, the new draft constitution proposes to create a category of serious cross-border crimes (for example, corruption, fraud and child-trafficking) that could be pursued by a European prosecutor.[56] Presumably, such a move would also require standardization of national criminal codes dealing with these specific felonies. It also seems likely that the draft constitution will seek expand to expand the EU's powers in the areas of immigration and internal security, two policy areas that have hitherto been too politically sensitive for Brussels to touch.

Notwithstanding, the obstacles to creation of a United States of Europe are formidable. One of the biggest obstacles also happens to one of the biggest member-states, namely the United Kingdom. Hence, "Britain, which is skeptical about creating anything that looks like a European state, is demanding the absolute right for any member nation to veto decision on foreign policy and taxation."[57] This is not to say that British government and society are opposed to the European Community (the first pillar), which both official policy and opinion polls show to be false. But the British, having so far remained out of the Euro zone, remain deeply skeptical of efforts to go beyond economic integration into realms that are not clearly related to the internal market. The British were among the delegations at Brussels that objected to the inclusion of the word "federal" to describe the way the union would function.[58] The draft approved at Brussels and presented at the EU summit in Greece substituted such innocuous phrases as "united in an ever closer union" for the unmentionable "f" word.[59]

The trans-Atlantic dispute over Iraq in 2003 mentioned above pitted the United States, backed primarily by Great Britain and Spain, against France, Germany and (to a lesser extent) Belgium. In addition, Poland sided with the United States, while Turkey balked at letting Washington use its territory as a springboard for the invasion. Nothing in recent years has cast the EU's lack of a foreign policy into sharper relief than the bitter dispute in the "Atlantic Community" and within the EU itself over war against Iraq. The significance of this episode for Europe is not what changed as a result of Washington's willingness to act without or without its European allies but rather what did not change.

Before moving on to a discussion of the EU and the United States, I will try to distill the essence of the dilemma facing Europe at the crossroads where it now finds itself. Europeans understand that the world has changed and that, in a real sense, it left the former Great Powers behind. Spain was the first to fall by the wayside centuries ago. Austria lost its place at the table of Great Power after World War I. Russia temporarily vacated its place as well. Great Britain and France fell into second-rank status as a consequence of World War II, while Germany was utterly defeated and occupied. That left only a resurgent Russia (in the guise of the Soviet Union) as a first-rank power in Europe. There was only one other first-rank power in the world, of course: the United States.

Recalling that the world from 1945 to 1989 was "bipolar" is not to belabor the obvious because now that the Cold War is over it is so easily overlooked. The legacy of that era remains deeply etched in the face of politics and public opinion in contemporary Europe. The very existence of the European Union is conspicuous evidence of Europe's continuing quest for a place in the new world order; its search for an alternative to the "war system" that had twice turned the Continent into a blood-drenched battlefield between 1914 and 1945; and its recognition that at a minimum peace and prosperity depend on economic integration. Paradoxically, the experience of the EU also illustrates the nation-state's lingering hold on hearts and minds of Europeans, including many who embrace the internal market (economic unity) but remain deeply attached to the symbols of substance of sovereignty (including the national flag, anthem, military forces, police, courts, diplomatic corps, foreign policy, and the like).

There are at least two other factors that touch a very sensitive national nerve in every country: the currency and language. The way the EU handled the currency question says a lot about Europe's ambivalence toward Brussels as a node of authority. In order to move the internal market forward, it was necessary to create a single currency and a European Central Bank. But for that to happen the member-states had to agree unanimously to abolish existing national currencies *and to sell this idea to the voters back home.* In 1998, the European Central Bank opened its doors in Frankfurt, Germany and eleven EU countries formally launched the Economic and Monetary Union (EMU) and began using the new euro. Significantly, four countries – Great Britain, Denmark, Sweden, and Greece – chose to stay out of the EMU. All 15 member-states agreed on at least one thing: respect for national authority (sovereignty) dictated that on a measure of such high emotional and political impact member-states must be allowed to stay out of the EMU without being evicted from the "club." The EU also refrained from creating a European Finance Minister because any such proposal would undoubtedly have met with strong resistance from many quarters.[60]

The language issue will perhaps be the most insuperable obstacle of all to the creation of a single Europe. It is one thing to take orders from a new boss; it is quite another thing to take orders from a new boss who does not even speak your language. Nothing illustrates the emotional side of politics more vividly than the language question. In the United States, the idea of bilingual education, for example, is extremely controversial. The famous American "melting pot" effect owes much to the fact that immigrants soon discover they cannot succeed unless they learn English.

A crucial difference between the United States of America and the potential United States of Europe is that the citizens of the new Europe are not immigrants. They have not chosen to leave family and friends, to seek a new life in a new land, to learn a new language and new way of seeing things. On this issue, France is one of the most adamant about the importance of preserving its national identity. (See Box "Tongue Tied in Europe") One senior French official at EU headquarters in Brussels put the matter succinctly: "It's not so much a single language that I fear but the single way of thinking that it brings with it."[61] The language issue threatens to rekindle the ancient cross-channel rivalry between the British and the French. For several centuries, French, not English, was the diplomatic language of Europe. It has also been the main language of the EU – until recently. Now French is being challenged by English within the EU as a result of the addition of two new Nordic members-states (Sweden and Finland) in 1995 and the 10 expansion states in 2004. Far more of the new Eurocrats from these countries will speak English than French as a second language. This trend will likely accelerate given the fact that "over 92 percent of secondary-school students in the EU's non-English-speaking countries are studying English, compared with 33 percent learning French and 13 percent studying German."[62]

Tongue-Tied in Europe

"The desire to protect and promote its language is a threat that runs through France's policy in the Union. For instance, longstanding efforts to develop a common EU patent-law have been stymied because France cannot accept English as the sole language for patents; and if French is made valid for EU patents, then the Germans, Italians and Spanish insist that their tongues should also be included. France has also consistently fought to prevent the EU gaining control of trade policy relating to 'cultural industries', lest this impede efforts to protect French-language films and music. And the French government has keenly championed Romania as a candidate to join the Union because of 'la Francophonie'....

The more realistic French officials acknowledge that however much cash and energy are put into the promotion of French within the Union and elsewhere, it is a losing battle. 'This is a real trauma for France,' says Mr [Bruno] Dethomas [one-time spokesman for former EU Commission president Jacques Delors]. 'Our only revenge is that the English language is being killed by all these foreigners speaking it so badly.'"

Charlemagne, "The galling rise of English," *The Economist*, March 31, 2003, p. 50.

Ambitious young Europeans are often keen to get a degree from a British or American university, where they are obviously exposed to ideas many Europeans consider anathema. The French official quoted earlier, for example, questions whether "it is possible to speak English without thinking American."[63]

France is the most vocal on this issue, but it is certainly not alone in wishing to protect its linguistic heritage. Czechs, for example, are not averse to learning foreign languages, but are often impatient with foreigners in their midst who do not speak Czech. Foreigners who take up temporary residence in the Czech Republic are often chided (and occasionally humiliated) for not speaking Czech or not speaking it well enough.[64] No doubt the point is equally valid for most of the other EU member-states.[65]

To summarize the main argument in this section, most Europeans today, including many who support the EU as presently constituted, would strongly oppose the creation of a European superstate.[66] A solid majority in the United Kingdom, Denmark, and possibly elsewhere, would also oppose any steps they believed might *eventually lead* to creation of a federal Europe. Yet there is a sophisticated and persistent cross-national minority of "federalists" and Eurocrats who, in the words of the 1957 Treaty of Rome Treaty, favor "ever closer union." In the words of one prominent Euro-federalist:

> ...the antidote to nationalism and chauvinism whether based on race or class, and ultimately to the totalitarian dictatorships which are its inevitable product in this century, is to hold federalist beliefs and put them into practice. It is to establish unity in diversity, an organic balance between local freedoms and communal obligations, and the pooling of "sovereign" rights which none of our countries is able to exercise alone in the present-day world.[67]

But, although the heirs of Jean Monnet will keep the hope of one Europe alive, the reality of Charles de Gaulle's *Europe des patries* shows no signs of fading any time soon. In short, Europe will not imitate the American "model" of federalism because it cannot and because Europe has always been about exploration and discovery – Europe innovates, it does imitate. In addition, Europeans continue to be highly ambivalent about Americans, admiring America's wealth and power but disdaining what they see as America's lack of cultural sophistication, its crass commercialism, its political immaturity, and, in recent times, its trigger-happy use of military force. Nonetheless, the Europe of the twenty-first century will be very different from the one America rescued in World War II. It is no longer artificially divided, the EU will continue to expand, and it will vie for bragging rights as the world's largest and most dynamic single economy. As promised, we now turn to the question of where and how the United States fits into this picture.

Europe and America

One of history's ironies is that the United States came into the world wanting to break away from Europe in the eighteenth century, endeavored to keep Europe out of the Western Hemisphere (the Monroe Doctrine) in the nineteenth century, and was pulled back into Europe in the twentieth century. After World War II, with Soviet dictator Josef Stalin's massive armies poised and forward-based in Poland and East Germany, the United States vowed to defend democracy in the part of Europe it had liberated by defeating another dictator, Adolph Hitler. In 1949, Washington institutionalized that commitment, creating the North Atlantic Treaty Organization (NATO), which bound the United States and the democracies of Western Europe in a new "Atlantic Community." American military muscle and West European weakness made this so-called "community" possible and fear of an imminent Soviet bid for hegemony in Europe made the NATO alliance necessary. In effect, the United States assumed the burden of Western Europe's defense after World War II because the war-devastated economies of the Continent were not capable of taking it on themselves. The American strategy was two-pronged: to stimulate a rapid economy recovery (hence the Marshall Plan in 1948) through an infusion of foreign aid and to promote economic prosperity through trade liberalization and, ultimately, creation of a large market similar to that in the United States. Thus, Washington encouraged the Schumann Plan (ECSC) and the Treaty of Rome (Common Market) in the 1950s, while maintaining a strong military presence in Germany and Italy, as well as the North Atlantic and the Mediterranean.

For the duration of the Cold War, two international organizations – the European Community (EC) and NATO – framed interstate relations within the Atlantic Community. It was a paradox of historic proportions that the success of the one made Western Europe an economic powerhouse at the same time that the other perpetuated its military weakness. So long as American taxpayers were willing to protect Western Europe (and pick up most of the tab), America's NATO allies had little incentive to invest heavily in their own defense. The fact that the US assumed the burden of Japan's defense after World War II, freeing Japan to concentrate on economic expansion and flood foreign markets with its exports, is frequently remarked. That the United States performed much the same service for Western Europe is often overlooked.[68]

The United States spent unprecedented sums during the formative first decades of the Cold War, prompting this admonition from President Dwight Eisenhower: "The problem in defense spending is to figure how far you should go without destroying from within what you are trying to defend from without." US military expenditures absorbed 9-10 percent of the total federal budget in the 1950s and 1960s, fell to about 5 percent in the post-Vietnam gloom of the 1970s, and climbed again to around 6 percent in the 1980s. "And in real terms it ran at $400 billion annually, in 1996 dollars, during Korea, Vietnam, and the second half of the 1980s, when it contributed to overall budget deficits."[69]

In hindsight, it is clear that one of the ironic consequences of the decision to create NATO – whether intended or unintended – was to insure that Western Europe would remain weak militarily *because* the United States was strong. "Free Europe" knew that Washington would come to its defense in a crisis (as it had already done twice in the first half of the twentieth century). In exchange Washington insisted on a dominant role in all matters affecting trans-Atlantic security (NATO's supreme commander is always an American). Western Europe, not unlike Japan, also benefited from being able to spend far less on defense than the United States was (and is) spending. America's NATO allies rarely spend more than 3 percent of GNP on defense; in the 1990s, this figure fell to around 2 percent on average, and for Germany it was only 1.5 percent. In 2003, the US military budget "exceeds the total military budgets of the world's next 14 biggest defense spenders put together."[70]

The enlarged EU is bigger by far than the United States demographically. It is roughly America's equal economically. The EU's military *potential* is thus enormous but its member-states, collectively speaking, command only modest military capabilities (see

31

Table 1.3). The reason is no mystery: They spend a combined total of about $140 billion on defense. By comparison, US military spending in 2003 will probably fall somewhere in the range of $400 billion. What this means in relative terms is that Americans will be spending almost three times as much on defense as Europeans. In research and development, the Pentagon spends $28,000 per soldier annually – four times more than Europe spends.[71]

Table 1.3
The European Balance of Power, 2000

	Potential Power		Actual Power	
	GNP (trillions $)	Population	Size of Army	Number of Nuclear Warheads
UK	1.26	59 million	301,150	185
France	1.47	59 million	411,800	470
Germany	2.20	82 million	516,500	0
Italy	1.16	58 million	164,900	0
Russia	0.33	147 million	348,000	10,000

Sources: GNP and Population figures are from World Bank Atlas 2000 (Washington, D.C., World Bank, April 2000), pp. 24-25, and 42-43. Figures for army size are from IISS, Military Balance, 2000/2001, pp. 58, 61, 67, 80, 120-21. Figures on nuclear weapons are from Robert S. Norris and William M. Arkin, "French and British Nuclear Forces, 2000" and "Russian Nuclear Forces, 2000," *Bulletin of the Atomic Scientists* 56, No. 5 (September-October 2000), pp. 69-71.

One prominent scholar argues that this wide divergence in military capabilities naturally created a difference in "strategic cultures" and in the theoretical framework of foreign policy in Europe and America. Americans, in this view, tend to see problems as black and white and the world politics as a contest between and evil. Europeans believe they are more sophisticated and see nuances that Americans often fail to see. Americans tend to be impatient and given to military action, whereas Europeans take a longer view, are more inclined to negotiate rather than fight, and trust persuasion more than coercion as an approach to problem-solving.[72]

Europe's inability to act independently on the world stage or to stand up to the United States was on display when a US (backed by the UK) invaded Iraq in 2003. France, Germany, Belgium and Turkey opposed the American decision, which they considered premature. Secretary of Defense Donald Rumsfeld expressed the anger of the Bush Administration when he disparaged France and Germany as the "old Europe."

But are these once-great powers really over the hill? France and Germany rank third and fourth in the world, economically, behind only the United States and Japan. They have a combined population of about 141 million, roughly equivalent to that of Russia. Germany and France together are the sheet anchor of the EU, which is only slightly behind the United States in the race to be the world's largest single economy.

And what of Great Britain? Certainly British military power cannot be discounted. Neither can the United States automatically count on it. The British under Prime Minister British Tony Blair have been solidly in the American camp in the war on terrorism and Iraq. But it is folly to assume that London will always choose the United States over Europe. There are strong historic and economic forces at work pulling Great Britain deeper and deeper into Europe's single economy.

Finally, Russia is a wild card in the new Europe. With the Czech Republic, Hungary, Poland, and the Slovak Republic poised to enter the EU in 2004, any trace of the old Iron Curtain that separated the Soviet Empire (Stalinist Russia and its vast fringe territories) from the West. In addition, the Baltic States, formerly part of the Soviet Union, will also join the EU in 2004. Russia is an economic midget, but a nuclear giant. (See Table 1.3) Russia's economy, still staggering after decades of Stalinist mismanagement, has shown some signs of turning around. Most economists agree that what it needs most of all is the strong medicine of competition – the kind of "therapy" the EU is tailored to administer.

So far, Russia is content to remain on the outside, but that, too, could change. Does it sound preposterous to suggest that Russia might apply for membership in the EU at some point? Perhaps. But not long ago it would have sounded no less preposterous to suggest that the Soviet Union would break up, that democracy would replace Stalinist dictatorship in Eastern Europe, and that the Cold War itself would become history.

Should the United States begin to take steps to wean Europe away from its dependency on American military protection now that the East-West conflict has ended? Europe does have the material wealth, human resources, and technological know-how to defend itself. To be sure, a militarily self-reliant, economically unified and solidly democratic Europe, would pose a challenge to the United States, but probably not a threat. Quite on the contrary, such a Europe would be a far better strategic partner for the United States, more capable of managing conflicts in its own backyard with or without US involvement, and able to share the burden of conflict management beyond the frontiers of Europe.[73] Such a Europe would not require (nor desire) a continued American troop presence. At the same time, by becoming more America's equal on the power scales, Europe might come to see the world more as Americans see it – namely as an arena where anarchy rules and the ever-present potential for conflict requires vigilance and a powerful punch.

Will the United States and an enlarged European Union become rivals rather than partners? Rivals, probably not; competitors, without a doubt. As the European Union has evolved and expanded, the trade disputes between Brussels and Washington have multiplied. Some of the most widely publicized sources of friction are connected with agriculture, a political "hot potato" on both sides of the Atlantic. Here are some examples of recent EU-US disputes in the headlines:

- US imposes "safeguard" duties on steel imports from the EU.

- EU protests the new U.S. farm bill as "protectionist."

- EU wins a $4 billion judgment against the U.S. "Foreign Sales Corporation" over tax provisions aimed at helping U.S. exporters.

- US challenges the EU's Common Agricultural Policy

- US denounces Airbus subsidies

- EU bans US biotech commodity exports

- US calls for the removal of "non-scientifically based barriers" to U.S. biotech commodity exports.

These differences are real and not easily resolved. Nonetheless, they have not led to a trans-Atlantic trade war. Why not? For the simple reason that both sides have way too much at stake. The EU is dependent on the US militarily, but the EU and US are *interdependent* economically.

The EU's military dependency is a condition that could eventually change; the same cannot be said of trans-Atlantic economic interdependency. The value of two-way trade and investment each year now totals some $2 trillion dollars. In the words of one high-ranking US trade official:

> It grows steadily and is usually quite balanced, affected only by business cycle trends on both sides of the Atlantic. Our capital markets are closely linked and increasingly integrated. European companies own firms we consider American icons such as Chrysler, Shell, Brooks Brothers, or Burger King. American firms own and are building viable futures for such European firms as Jaguar and Volvo.[74]

The market-based economies of Europe and North America are intermeshed in ways that go well beyond trade policies and inter-state relations, it is true, but there are some signs of a loosening of trans-Atlantic economic ties as well. Hence, the relative importance of the EU as a market for American goods has steadily declined over the past 20 years, from a peak of more than 30 percent in 1982 to slightly less than 12 percent in 2001.[75] This shift reflects the rapid growth of US farm exports to Canada and Mexico in the 1990s following the birth of the North American Free Trade Association (NAFTA), and to East Asia, as well as an overall drop in exports to the EU.

Nonetheless, US agricultural imports from the EU reached a historic peak of $8.1 billion in 2000, resulting in an agricultural trade deficit with EU of some $1.8 billion.[76] The picture was basically unchanged through 2001, but a falling US stock market, weakening dollar, and faltering economy in 2002-2003 reduced demand for imports and gave US exports a boost, illustrating the extent to which trans-Atlantic trade relations are subject to the vicissitudes of the larger world economy and market forces.

In a recent issue of *Foreign Affairs*, a prominent US economist remarks on "the mammoth size of U.S. exports to East Asia" and notes, in 2001, "precisely a quarter of United States' total exports of goods went to the Pacific Rim."[77] The value of these exports totaled a stunning $182 billion, which "was identical to the value of the United States' exports to Europe." In 2002 the share of US merchandise exports to the Pacific Rim (26 percent of the total) actually exceeded Europe's share (24 percent).[78]

Critics of US trade policy decry the growing "economic regionalism" in the global economy.[79] They argue that Washington gave this trend a big boost by creating NAFTA in the early 1990s. At present, 37 percent of US merchandise exports go to Mexico and Canada, more than to Europe or Asia, but not by a huge margin. By contrast, two-thirds of exports from EU member-state stay within European Union, and Japan's exports are similarly concentrated in the Asian region.[80] These facts point to the regionalism itself is becoming a global issue. If so, the implications for the European Union and the "trans-Atlantic community" could be enormous. In the final section, I summarize my main points and draw some conclusions about the EU's prospects for the future.

Summary and Conclusions

From the standpoint of peace and stability, as well as economic prosperity, the European Union is an unprecedented achievement. No previous effort at inter-state cooperation can compare in scope and duration. In the space of half a century, the world has witnessed an experiment involving 6 West European states joined in a limited partnership for coal and steel in 1953 evolve into a massive single market encompassing 25 states from the Arctic Circle (Sweden and Finland) to the Mediterranean (Malta and Cyprus).

The dream of a united Europe, however, is not new. For centuries, theologians and philosophers have imagined a Europe united by common religious and cultural values. But the ideal of unity was repeatedly thwarted by the reality of a Europe divided against itself by the forces of nationalism reified in the nation-state system. War, not reason or the rule of law, was final arbiter in this system. Three total wars in a century and half ultimately destroyed the classical balance of power system in Europe. In the process, these wars – beginning with Napoleon Bonaparte's bid for hegemony and ending with Adolph Hitler's – demonstrated the futility of resorting to arms. It also left the former great powers (with the exception of Soviet Russia) weakened, vulnerable and dependent on a non-European upstart for succor and security.

The secret of Europe's success has been its vitality and dynamism. Here is one of history's great paradoxes: The same competitive energy that produced frequent conflicts on the Continent also powered the Renaissance, the Age of Discovery, and the Scientific Revolution. It is significant that the explorers who first set sail in the 15th century to map the world also set the stage for its conquest by Europeans armed with superior weapons.[81]

Europe's competitive drive, however, was also its downfall. Europe's intrusion into the New World led to the birth of the United States, which is now far superior in economic and military prowess to any of the former great powers that once colonized North America (Russia, Spain, France, and Great Britain). Indeed, today the United States is superior to all of them put together.

Not only is America economically and military superior to Europe today, but Asia is also dynamic and growing rapidly. Japan, not France or Germany, is now the second largest economic power in the world (despite setbacks and an overall slowdown in recent years). China, with a huge internal market of its own, is growing at a much faster rate than Europe. South Korea is back on track after a financial crisis rippled through Asia in the late 1990s. The prospect of an all-Asia regional free trade area (FTA) that includes Japan, as well as China and South Korea, poses a major challenge to the EU (as well as the US).[82] Meanwhile, the European Union has moved forward in fits and starts but its economic performance has left something to be desired.

How will the EU cope with the intensely competitive global environment of the future? Only time will tell, but it is safe to say how the EU will not cope, or rather, what it will not do anytime soon. It will not re-make itself in the image of its trans-Atlantic patron – it will not become the United States of Europe.[83] The genius of Europe is about artistic creation and technological innovation, not imitation.

The EU will continue to expand until it has incorporated all the countries of Europe that wish to join. Very likely that will exclude a few, such as Switzerland and Norway where political tradition or public sentiment or special circumstances militate against the idea. A big question for the future is what to do about two big countries on the periphery – Russia and Turkey. There are strong arguments for including both: Russia is part of Europe and Turkey is part of NATO with a long historic presence in Europe (the Balkans).[84] Admitting those two countries alone would add more than 210 million people to the EU's already prodigious market. It would also add the military strength of two large armies and the world's second largest nuclear arsenal.

But admitting Russia would also lead the EU into perilous and uncharted waters because Moscow has a short and troubled democratic tradition; because it has always favored autarky in its economic policies; because its economy lags far behind the EU norm; and because its vast Asian territories and as yet unresolved "national minorities" question (for example, Chechnya) would likely bring a whole new set of problems to Brussels doorstep. Similarly, Turkey is part of Asia geographically and has close religious and cultural ties to the Middle East. If the EU opens its doors to Turkey, why not admit Morocco or even Israel? Thus, one of the important questions on the EU agenda for the future will be where and how to draw the line, both geographically and politically.

Economically, the EU is committed to a single market and there is no strong dissent or debate over this question. Eventually, even the United Kingdom will most likely join the Euro zone and there will be a single currency and a single set of monetary and fiscal policies for all. But it is mistaken to draw the line between economics and politics too sharply. In fact, there is bound to be spillover from the economic sphere to the political: economic coordination requires political accommodation which, in turn, will put Europe's national political cultures in competition with an emerging regional political culture. Over time, it is possible (though by no means certain) that a European identify will emerge. Only then will the age-old idea of political union become a possibility.

Until that distant time, however, politics in Europe will continue to bear the imprint of nation-states. There will not be any dramatic political breakthrough within the European Union nor will there be a break down. Instead, the EU will continue to muddle through, impeded by its cumbersome decision-making machinery but not altogether stymied by it either. Even in the best of circumstances, it seems unlikely that Europe in the twenty-first century will regain the leadership role it lost in the twentieth century. The question is not whether Asia can catch up but whether Europe can keep up.

Select Bibliography

Calleo, David. Europe's Future: The Grand Alternatives. New York: Norton. 1967.

de Rougemont, Denis. The Meaning of Europe. New York: Stein and Day, 1965.

Dinan, Desmond. Ever Closer Union. 2d. ed. Boulder, Colo.: Lynne Rienner, 1999.

Magstadt, Thomas. 4th ed. Nations and Governments: Comparative Politics in Regional Perspective. Boston & New York: Bedford/St.Martin's, 2002.

Moravcsik, Andrew. The Choice for Europe. Ithaca, N.Y.: Cornell University Press, 1998.

Peterson, John, and Bomberg, Elizabeth. Decision-Making in the European Union. New York: St. Martin's Press, 1999.

Rose, Richard. What Is Europe? New York: HarperCollins, 1996.

Tsoukalis, Loukas. The New European Economy Re-visited. Oxford: Oxford University Press, 1997.

Wallace, Helen, and Wallace, William. Policymaking in the European Union. 4th ed. Oxford: OxfordUniversity Press, 2000.

Wood, David and Yeşilada, Birol. The Emerging European Union. 2d.ed. New York: Longman, 2002.

Web Sites:

General EU Web site, *http://europa.eu.int/index_en.htm*.

Jean Monnet at Harvard Web site, *http://www.law.harvard.edu\programs\jeanmonnet\euatharvard*.

U.S. Department of State, European Affairs, *http://www.state.gov/www/regions/eur*.

Notes

[1] David Calleo, *Europe's Future: The Grand Alternatives* (New York: W.W. Norton, 1967), p. 23.
[2] Ibid.
[3] Ibid. pp. 25-16.
[4] Ibid.
[5] Ibid. p. 27.
[6] Denis de Rougemont, *The Meaning of Europe* (New York: Stein and Day, 1965), p. 68.
[7] Ibid. pp. 68-80.
[8] Ibid. p. 81. See also, Calleo, *Europe's Future*, pp. 29-32.
[9] Calleo, *Europe's Future*, pp. 31.
[10] Ibid.
[11] Ibid. (The author's citation of the complete text for this declaration is found on page 88.)
[12] Ibid. pp. 82-85.
[13] See, for example, Richard Rose, *What is Europe?* (New York: HarperCollins, 1996), pp. 12-17. The author posits that the state is still the pivotal feature of European politics and, while not denying the growing role of interdependence, notes "the politics of the European Union emphasizes disagreements." See also, Calleo, *Europe's Future*, pp. 35-36. A span of some thirty years separated the appearance of these books, but the two authors' assessment of Europe's prospects for federation are remarkably similar. Thus, Calleo wrote (p. 37): "While federalism as an ideal has gained many ardent enthusiasts in modern times, federalism as a process seeking to convert the national states into a new order has made little progress."
[14] It is this dynamism and sense of adventure that defines Europe, according to some scholarly observers. See, for example, de Rougement, *Meaning of Europe*, pp. 11-28.
[15] Ibid. pp. 17-24.
[16] Known as the Fouchet Plan, this arrangement would have institutionalized regular meetings among European heads of state with the purpose of hammering out common policies "at the summit". For an excellent (and rather sympathetic) discussion of this idea, see Calleo, *Europe's Future*, pp. 128-133.
[17] Ibid. p. 74.
[18] Ibid. pp. 73-75.
[19] Ibid. p. 75
[20] Shirley William, "Sovereignty and Accountability in the European Community," in Robert O. Keohane and Stanley Hoffman, eds., *The New European Community: Decisionmaking and Institutional Change* (Boulder: Westview Press, 1991), pp. 175-176; see also, Juliet Lodge, "The European Parliament," in Sven S. Andersen and Kjell A. Eliassen, eds., *The European Union: How Democratic Is It?* (London: Sage Publications, 1996) pp. 187-214.
[21] Frank Bruni and Anthee Carassava, "For Europe, the Messages Differ on the State of the Union," *The New York Times*, [electronic edition], June 22, 2003.
[22] "Europe moves east," The World in 2003, *The Economist*, p. 14.
[23] Ibid.
[24] "Eurobarometer," *The Economist*, September 9, p. 2000. See also, Thomas M. Magstadt, *Nations and Governments* (Boston: Bedford/St. Martin's Press, 2002), p. 172.
[25] Calleo, *Europe's Future*, p. 81.
[26] Ibid.
[27] Ibid., p. 82. De Gaulle, according to Calleo, "has been unyieldingly hostile to the supranational pretensions of the Common Market, but he has energetically encourages European economic integration.... He would build Europe around the existing national states rather than a

new federal center. De Gaulle's union would week to coordinate national policies wherever possible while leaving the political sovereignty of the states intact."

[28] Ibid., pp. 85-86. De Gaulle made this observation in a press conference on February 25, 1953 at a time when his own political future, and that of France, was clouded and uncertain.

[29] Ibid., p. 87. Speech, November 4, 1951.

[30] Ibid. Press conference, December 21, 1951.

[31] Elaine Sciolino, "Seeking Unity, Europe Drafts a Constitution," *The New York Times* [electronic edition], June 15, 2003.

[32] Ibid. See also, "Tidying up or tyranny?" T*he Economist*, May 31, 2003, pp. 51-52.

[33] "Tidying up or tyranny," *The Economist*, May 31, 2003, pp. 51-52.

[34] Ibid.

[35] Ibid.

[36] Sciolino, "Seeking Unity..."

[37] Ibid. A British delegate to the Brussels convention and the European Parliament, Gisela Stuart, complained, "Right now, if my prime minister goes to Brussels and makes decisions behind closed doors, I as a parliamentarian cannot hold him to account because I only know the outcome, I don't know the process. It's the same with the ministers. They can tell me anything."

[38] Ibid. This question was actually posed by Giuliano Amato, the former Italian prime minister, who played a prominent role at the Brussels convention. A constitutional law expert, Giuliano favored merging the two presidencies in 2015 but it was an idea whose time had not come.

[39] Rose, *What is* Europe?, p. 40. Similarly, Calleo writes how "...to Frenchman long devoted to the European cause, Robert Schuman, the Foreign Minister, and Jean Monnet, the Father of Europe," produced what must surely be one of the most imaginative diplomatic solutions in modern history, the European Coal and Steel Community. It was impossible, they argued to tie together France and Germany through classical diplomatic arrangements. The basic problem was that neither could afford to concede much to the other without feeling its own security and prosperity endangered, and thus the old cycle of competition and fear had continued endlessly. The only solution was to fuse the two countries in such a way that each would lose its independent power to do mortal harm to the other. They could then cooperate without fearing that what benefited one invariably threatened the other." Calleo, *Europe's Future*, p. 48.

[40] For a recent analysis of the role of these factors in determining the power capabilities of the main actors in international politics, see John Mearsheimer, *The Tragedy of the Great Powers* (New York: Norton, 2001), pp. 55-82.

[41] See, David Mitrany, A Working Peace System (Chicago: Quadrangle Books, 1966). Mitrany developed the first comprehensive functionalist theory in the 1940s as a practical way use international organizations as vehicles for developing the habit of cooperation on the part of states far more accustomed to competition. For an analysis of the connection between the functionalists and European supranationalists see David Wood and Birol Yeşilada, *The Emerging European Union* (New York: Longman, 2002), pp 13-17.

[42] One exception is President Vaclav Klaus, former leader of the opposition center-right party in the Czech Republic, who expressed doubts prior to the national referendum in June 2003 saying that he thought Czechs deserved more time to enjoy sovereignty after a long period of Soviet tutelage prior to 1989. But even Klaus "the only leader of a candidate country not to strongly support membership has compared the outcome of the Czech vote to a lump of sugar dropped into a cup of coffee." See wire-service article, "Czechs Ratify EU Membership," *Washington Post*, June 15, 2003, p. A25.

[43] On this point, see Mark Kesselman and Joel Krieger, et.al., *Europeans Politics in Transition* (Boston: Houghton-Mifflin, 2002), p. 144-146. As the authors point out, the EU "is a promiscuity of different types of representation. National political elites...can skirt

accountability.... The Parliament does not engage the attention of those who elect it... There is no clear choice between parties on Europolicy lines.... The European Parliament may do good work analyzing and scrutinizing proposals sent to it, but very few people know about this work, and even fewer understand where it fits politically."

[44] "What a pity. What a relief," *The Economist*, June 14, 2003, p. 46.

[45] European Commission, *Eurobarometer: Public Opinion in the European Union* 53, October 2000, p. 8. Thirty-eight percent of Swedes expressed strong reservations about the EU in this survey.

[46] Ibid. Only 9 percent of Italians gave the thumbs down to the EU, compared to 14 percent of French, and 15 percent of Germans. These numbers are surprisingly low especially given the contentious issues the EU has faced in recent years.

[47] See, for example, "Back into the fold," *The Economist*, June 14, 2003, pp. 45-46.

[48] "Come on, try and get excited," *The Economist*, June 7, 2003, p. 45. Lithuania's referendum resulted in a resounding 91 percent yes vote with a 63 percent turnout

[49] According to Jeffrey Gedmin, director of the Berlin-based Aspen Institute, "The Germans will say that the union is like a bicycle, and if you don't keep pedaling forward, you fall off. The British will say that you can stop and park a bicycle from time to time without getting off it." Quoted in Frank Bruni and Anthee Carassava, "For Europe, the Messages Differ..."

[50] "Union Pauses for Breath," *The Economist*, February 12, 2002, p. 27.

[51] Charlemagne, "Snoring while a superstate emerges?, *The Economist*, May 10, 2003, p. 46. According to this article, Austrians estimated that 60-70% of their laws were being generated in Brussels, while a study by the *Conseil d'Etat* in Paris in the early 1990s put the figure for France at 55%.

[52] Ibid.

[53] Ibid.

[54] Ibid.

[55] Exactly how to give Brussels more central control in the area of border inspection without opening up a Pandora's box has apparently proved to be all-too perplexing. One scholar in the US has advocated the wholesale transfer of European security policy to the EU and even creation "if necessary [of] a single EU security service and border-control force." But having proposed this move, he then demonstrates unwittingly how unrealistic it is given the divergent views and interests of big states versus small states, and the like. See Barry Eichengreen, "Putting It Together: The Foibles and Future of the European Union," [Review Essay] *Foreign Affairs*, July/August 2003, pp.198-199.

[56] So-called "Eurosceptics" greeted the proposal to create a European Public Prosecutor with alarm. See, for example, "Nothing like good enough, so far," *The Economist*, May 31, 2003, p. 14.

[57] Sciolino, "Seeking Unity..."

[58] Frank Bruni and Anthee Carassava, "For Europe, the Messages Differ..." Thus, Prime Minister Costas Simitis of Greece said the evolving draft constitution reflected a shared belief in "a federal kind of Europe," while the British Prime Minister Tony Blair insisted it aimed at "a Europe of nations, not a federal superstate."

[59] Sciolini, "Seeking Unity."

[60] The new constitution also will apparently not address this issue, although some delegates to the Brussels convention favored it. See, "Your darkest fears addressed, your hardest questions answered," [Special report: Europe's constitution], *The Economist*, June 21, 2003, p. 52.

[61] Charlemagne, "The galling rise of English," *The Economist*, March 31, 2003, p. 50.

[62] Ibid.

[63] Ibid.

[64] As a Fulbright Lecturer in the Czech Republic in the mid-1990s, I speak from first-hand experience. Of course, Czechs have as much right to expect American visitors there to speak Czech as Americans do to expect foreigner visitors to speak English. The point here is simply that people everywhere have too much invested in their native tongue to give it up without a fight and that poses problems for a multi-lingual political entity like the EU.

[65] This observation has to be qualified because there are some exceptions – the Netherlands is virtually bilingual (Dutch and English), while Belgium has three official languages.

[66] As John Gillingham points out repeatedly in his recently published history of the European Union, the governments of the EU member-states reflect this popular sentiment and continue to resist proposals to pool sovereignty even on a limited basis. See, John Gillingham, *European Integration 1950-2002: Superstate or New Market Economy?* (New York: Cambridge University Press, 2003.).

[67] de Rougemont, *The Meaning of Europe*, p. 112.

[68] Japan spends on average only about 1 percent of its GNP on defense; the figure for Western Europe is closer to 3 percent.

[69] Jeremy Isaacs and Taylor Downing, *The Cold War: An Illustrated History* (New York: Little, Brown and Company, 1998), online at www.cnn.com/SPECIAL/cold.war/episodes/24/epilogue/.

[70] Steven Erlanger, "Military Gulf Separates U.S. and European Allies," *The New York Times* (online edition), March 16, 2002.

[71] Ibid.

[72] Robert Kagan, "Power and Weakness," *Policy Review*, No. 113, June/July 2002. The reader can find this article on line at www.policyreview.org. Kagan acknowledges his intellectual debt to John Harper (*American Visions of Europe*). However, Harper takes issue with Kagan's assessment of Western Europe's military weakness, which Harper thinks Kagan overstates. See his letter to the editor in *Policy Review*, No. 115, October-November, 2002.

[73] Erlanger, "Military Gulf." Erlanger reports, "European governments sense that they are increasingly becoming second-rank powers, unable to affect American foreign policy goals because they can bring too few assets to the table." He notes NATO's Secretary General, Lord Robertson, has warned Europeans they will have to choose "modernization or marginalization" and US Ambassador to NATO Nicholas Burns expressed fear that the alliance will become "so unbalanced that we may no longer have the ability to fight together in the future."

[74] Charles Ries, Principal Deputy Assistant Secretary for European and Eurasian Affairs, "The U.S.-EU Trade Relationship: Partners and Competitors." Speech in Miami, Florida, November 14, 2002 [on line at www.state.gov/p/eur/rls/rm/2002/1549/pf.htm].

[75] These figures are obtained from the ERS/USDA Briefing Room – European Union: Trade, Economic Research Service, US Department of Agriculture at www.ers.usda.gov/Briefing/EuropeanUnion/trade.htm accessed by the author on June 26, 2003.

[76] Ibid. The trade deficit resulted from a steady growth in overall farm imports in the 1990s.

[77] Bernard K. Gordon, "A High-Risk Trade Policy," *Foreign Affairs*, Volume 82, No. 4, July/August 2003, p. 109.

[78] Ibid.

[79] Ibid. This is the point of Gordon's article.

[80] Ibid., p. 111.

[81] See, for example, Jared Diamond, *Guns, Germs, and Steel: The Fate of Human Societies* (New York: Norton, 1997).

[82] Gordon, "A High-Risk Trade Policy," pp. 107-111.

[83] In the run-up to the constitutional convention in Brussels, a proposal to re-name the European Union the "United States of Europe" was floated but quietly dropped without debate – mute

testimony to the strong resistance against any hint that Europe might profit by mimicking America.

[84] See, for example, the cover story, "Turkey belongs in Europe," in *The Economist*, December 7, 2002, p. 13.